W9-AJP-870

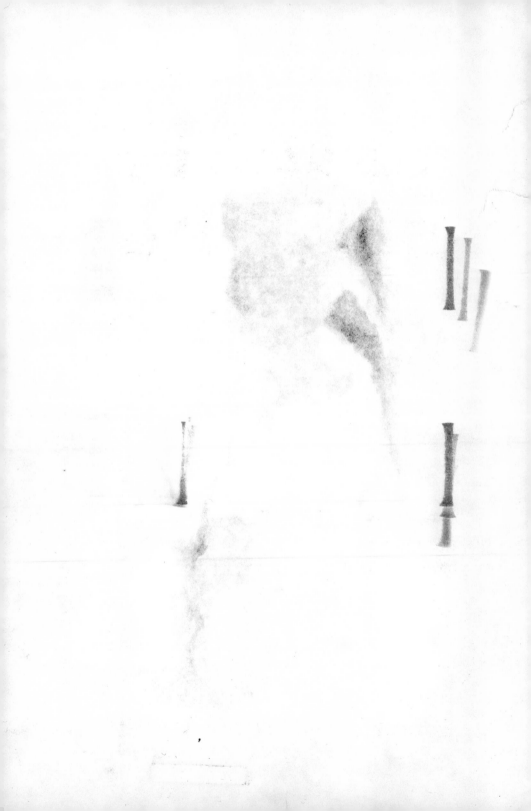

Choosing Your Pet

by Mark McPherson

photography by
Marianne Bernstein

EAU CLAIRE DISTRICT LIBRARY

_____Troll Associates

80741

4/24/86 Troll 9 89 -

Library of Congress Cataloging in Publication Data

McPherson, Mark (Mark D.)
   Choosing your pet.

   Includes index.
   Summary: Information on selecting and caring for many
kinds of pets, including rodents, cats, dogs, birds,
and fish.
   1. Pets—Juvenile literature. [1. Pets] I. Bernstein,
Marianne, ill.   II. Title.
SF416.2.M34   1984   636.08 '87   84-226
ISBN 0-8167-0111-3 (lib. bdg.)
ISBN 0-8167-0112-1 (pbk.)

Copyright © 1985 by Troll Associates
All rights reserved. No part of this book may be used or reproduced in any manner whatsoever without written
permission from the publisher. Printed in the United States of America. Troll Associates, Mahwah, N.J.

The author and publisher wish to thank the ASPCA of New York City, Akitas of Distinction of New York City, and Laura and Alexander
Spellman.

Photographs on pages 16, 21, 23, 27, 28 (right), 32, 37, 39, 40, 43, 45 by Aaron Norman. Photograph on page 18 by David W. White.

10   9   8   7   6   5   4   3   2   1

Contents

The Right Pet For You

Having a pet can be one of the best things in your life. A pet can be a friend and companion, a source of amusement and wonder.

But *every* pet also needs your help and your care. So when you start thinking about owning a pet, you also have to start thinking about where you will keep it, how much time you will be able to devote to it, and, finally, just what kind of pet will be right for you.

As you read this book you will learn about different kinds of animals that make good pets. There are mice and gerbils, dogs and cats, parrots and lizards, fish and turtles, and many more. As you find out what each pet requires from you—like

how often you must feed it or how often you must clean its cage—think carefully about how those responsibilities will affect you. Do you think that you can handle them? Will you be able to give your pet everything it needs?

For instance, do you have a back yard with a fence where a big dog could exercise? Or do you live in a city where a dog would depend on walks on a leash for all its exercise? Finally, what kinds of pets will your parents let you keep in the house?

It is important to sit down with your parents for a heart-to-heart talk. They'll want to know if you will meet your obligations to your pet. They will also want to know how much of their time will be required to help you out. And you will have to decide together on a pet the whole family will enjoy.

Once you have consulted with your parents and checked your own schedule, you will be ready to make a decision. This book will help you make a choice—whether you want to care for a pet as simple as a fish, as difficult as a dog, or something in between.

Make sure that you have time in your schedule to care for the pet you choose.

Mice, Hamsters, Gerbils, and Rats

Mice, hamsters, gerbils, and rats are all rodents and all four can be kept as pets. They are not geniuses, but they are much smarter than you might think. Once they get to know you and trust you, they will be friendly and often very cute.

All of these rodents have teeth that *grow*. They keep wearing their teeth down on the hard foods that they eat, and gnawing on things is one of their favorite activities.

Rodents also sleep during the day and are active at night. They are all burrowers, or diggers, who like to find dark, safe hiding places in their cages, just as they would if they were in the wild.

When you go to buy a rodent, you should get one that is very young, ideally four to six weeks old. This is the age at which a rodent is most likely to learn to feel at ease with people. The rodent you choose should be plump and have a shiny, smooth coat.

You will need a cage or a glass fish tank. Metal cages are much better than wooden or plastic ones, because they stop the rodent from gnawing its way out. A medium-sized rodent cage or a five-and-a-half gallon fish tank will do. You will also need a weighted-down, wire-mesh top for the cage, a water bottle, and wood shavings for bedding (and to absorb urine).

MICE

An uninvited mouse in your house is a nuisance. But a pet mouse can be fun. Mice have lots of energy and are always moving, sniffing around, and eating.

Most pet mice are white, but they can also be gray, brown, black, or spotted. Although mice are cute, they are also nervous. They are real escape artists, and once they escape, they are good at staying hidden.

Of the four rodents you might choose for pets, mice are the ones whose cages must be cleaned most often. That is because they have the strongest-smelling urine. Having strong-smelling urine does not make them bad pets. It just means that their cages need to be cleaned at least once, preferably twice a week. A mouse keeps itself clean and doesn't ever need a bath.

It is easy to provide for a mouse's diet. They like gerbil food and birdseed. For treats, mice also enjoy small pieces of vegetables, uncooked grains, peanut butter, or cheese. They will appreciate a bone for leisure-time gnawing.

Mice are a little nervous, but really cute.

HAMSTERS

Hamsters are cuddly-looking, plump, and a bit grouchy. They need to be carefully and gently tamed when they are young, and someone who owns a hamster must know when not to bother it.

A hamster sleeps soundly, usually during the day. It wakes up slowly and may give a little nip if disturbed. But when well-tamed, a hamster is playful and friendly.

Most of the time it is awake, a hamster will run on its exercise wheel. It will also hoard food in secret corners of its cage. To keep its home clean, find out where the hamster hides its food and remove it from the cage from time to time.

Pet stores sell hamster food that is made up of seeds, grain, and dried fruit. You can add small amounts of fruit and vegetables to their diet.

Time and patience will make hamsters tame and friendly pets.

GERBILS

The gerbil is a native of the desert. It has brown, oily fur and a long, furry tail.

One nice thing about a gerbil is that it is friendlier than a hamster. Another nice thing is that a gerbil's cage rarely gets smelly. You will probably need to clean the cage only once a month. A gerbil makes very little urine because its body uses almost all of the water that it drinks.

A gerbil tends to be a little nervous, but it puts a lot of its energy into digging in the bottom of its cage (and throwing wood shavings all over).

You can buy gerbil food in pet stores. On occasion, add some oatmeal, peanut butter, and fresh vegetables to the gerbil's diet.

A gerbil's natural home is the desert.

RATS

A pet rat is the smartest as well as the friendliest of the four rodents you may want to consider for a pet. The only problem with a rat is its image. Many people say "yecck" when they hear the word "rat." But a rat sold as a pet is a far cry from the wild rat that scares people.

Most pet rats are white, although some are black, or black and white. A pet rat is much smaller than a wild rat, and it lacks the aggressive, frightening nature of its wild cousin.

A pet rat is usually quite calm and is an enthusiastic explorer who won't run away and hide when you let it out of its cage. It's a better pet than a mouse, hamster, or gerbil. The rat will also remember who feeds it and will not be shy about

Rats are the most intelligent of the rodents that you can keep as pets.

11

begging for food at every opportunity.

A rat eats a wide variety of foods. A combination of gerbil food, birdseed, guinea pig food, and rabbit food provides a good basic diet. But rats also enjoy small quantities of fruit, vegetables, nuts, chicken bones, meat, and grains.

Always keep a rodent's cage clean. Rats are the most intelligent of the rodents that you can keep as pets.

Rabbits and Guinea Pigs

If you would like a larger pet than a mouse, hamster, gerbil, or rat, you may be happy with a guinea pig or a rabbit.

A pet rabbit or guinea pig should be kept in a hutch, a large cage. If kept indoors, the hutch sits over several layers of newspapers. Droppings and urine fall through the wire bottom of the hutch onto the paper, which you must change at least twice a week. If you keep the rabbit hutch outdoors, you can move it from time to time so that the valuable fertilizer is spread around the yard.

RABBITS

Get a rabbit when it is young, eight weeks or a little older. Handle it daily, let it get used to

Rabbits become friendly, loyal pets.

13

EAU CLAIRE DISTRICT LIBRARY

Lettuce and carrots are among a rabbit's favorite treats.

you, and it should turn into a first-class pet.

Rabbits available in pet stores weigh about four pounds full-grown. When selecting a baby rabbit, look for one that is a little plump. It should have thick fur that is also a bit shiny. Make sure that it has neither runny eyes nor a runny nose. It is usually best to have just one rabbit, since grown-up rabbits do not get along well together in a hutch.

The friendliest pet rabbits will become attached to you, occasionally follow you around, and expect generous amounts of petting. Once a week use a dog brush to groom a rabbit. Brush more often when the rabbit is shedding. In warm weather, your rabbit will shed heavily.

Rabbit pellets, sold in pet stores, are the most important part of a rabbit's diet. A rabbit will usually enjoy a nice carrot, as well as lettuce, cabbage leaves, and grass clippings from a lawn that has not been sprayed with weed killer.

A rabbit also drinks a lot of water and needs a greater amount of salt than most animals. Purchase a salt lick from a pet store and put it in the hutch. The rabbit will take the salt it needs.

GUINEA PIGS

Purchase baby guinea pigs when they are around one month old. If you want one that will be easier to tame, try to get a guinea pig that is calm. Handle the baby guinea pig as often as possible so that it loses its fear of being around people.

Guinea pigs are not as smart as rabbits. They don't come looking for petting, but they do respond with a kind of purr to a gentle rubbing behind the ears. They are called "pigs" because of the sounds they make, which resemble the oinks and snorts of real pigs.

A guinea pig loves to eat. It also shares one thing in common with monkeys and humans that other animals do not. A guinea pig does not produce its own vitamin C. That is one reason why it requires its own guinea pig pellets, which resemble rabbit pellets, but also contain Vitamin C. In addition to guinea pig pellets, feed your guinea pig fresh vegetables and fruits that are high in vitamin C. Like a rabbit, a guinea pig will also enjoy grass clippings or hay and appreciate a salt lick in its hutch.

Guinea pigs are not very smart, but they try.

Cats

If you want an independent pet, a cat or a kitten is the perfect choice.

Cats and people go back a long way, at least to ancient Egypt, where cats were thought to be gods. Today they come in a variety of breeds, or types.

The easiest way to obtain a kitten is by looking for advertisements in a local newspaper or on a bulletin board. There are usually far more

Cats always look like they know more than they are willing to tell.

kittens up for adoption than there are people to adopt them. Choose carefully, and do not lose your heart to the first cute kitten you meet.

Kittens that are healthy and have been handled by humans make the best pets. A playful, responsive kitten is the right choice over a nervous, timid kitten. A good kitten will be calm in your arms after you have picked it up. If the kitten cannot relax after you have petted it gently, then it

Above: Put a kitten into a litter box, and it will use it from then on. Left: When a kitten is handled with love, it will get used to people.

may not make a good pet. Pick up another kitten from the litter to see how it responds. You do not want a cat that does not like people from the start.

Take the kitten home after it is weaned (when it no longer needs its mother's milk) at around two months of age. At this early stage, your new kitten will appreciate at least three daily meals. Gradually reduce these feedings to one meal a day by the time your once-tiny kitten is a young cat.

In addition to fresh water each day, all that a cat needs is the regular cat food sold in grocery stores, particularly the dry chow. A special treat like beef liver is fine once in a while.

When you pick up your kitten to take it home, find out if it has already been taken to a veterinarian (an animal doctor) for shots. Learn which shots it received, if any. As soon as possible, take the kitten to the vet to have it checked for worms, given shots against disease, and generally examined.

While at the vet's, ask about spaying (for female kittens) and neutering (for male kittens). Unless you want a female to have kittens of her 17

Lounging around is a favorite cat activity. Does this cat look like it has any problems?

own, it is wise to have her spayed. It is also a good idea to have a male neutered.

One of the nicest things about cats is that they are clean animals. There is hardly any work at all in housebreaking a cat. All the cat needs is a place to dig and bury. Just fill up a litter box with litter and show the cat where it is. Try to scoop droppings out of the litter box every day. Change the litter and wash the box out once a week.

There are some other important things to remember about cat care. Cats need to be brushed, especially if they are long-haired and when they are shedding. It is also wise to give them something on which to scratch their nails. A log, nailed upright on a square plywood base, makes a good scratching post. Many pet stores sell scratching posts that are covered with carpet scraps.

A cat can become a great pet and an important member of your household. Cats are intelligent and independent, and easy to care for.

Canaries and Parakeets

Canaries and parakeets are small, beautiful birds. Sometimes they can sing, and sometimes they can be trained to perch on your finger. But you must be patient.

Both canaries and parakeets are affordable and easy to care for. In your home they will have to live in cages. This may bother you if you've always thought of birds as being free to fly wherever and whenever they please. Yet living in your house in a cage is safer than living outdoors.

When selecting a bird, make sure you don't purchase one that is sick. Feathers should lie full and flat. Ruffles or bald spots are a sign of illness. A healthy bird should appear a little nervous. Flying a bit in its cage when bothered is another good sign. A bird that seems calm and passive may really be too weak to be frightened. A

Pet birds need a daily supply of birdseed. This cage has a feeder in its base that pulls out like a drawer.

bird's eyes should be clear, giving the appearance of alertness, and feathers should be clean, particularly under the tail where evidence of droppings may indicate sickness.

CANARIES

Canaries are prized for their singing and their beauty. It is only the male canary that sings, however. Since just looking at the bird will not tell you the difference between a male and female, get a guarantee in writing from the pet store. If you don't care whether or not a canary will sing, then just pick one you like that shows the signs of good health.

A canary for sale should have a band

Canaries are prized for their songs, but only male canaries sing.

around its leg that reports its age. A male will begin to sing after six months of age. By one year it should have a fully developed song.

PARAKEETS

With patience and a little persistence on your part, a parakeet can become a devoted pet.

Before you can tame a parakeet, it must get used to the idea that it will be handled. Begin the process by resting your hand quietly at the door of its cage (canaries are tamed in the same way).

Naturally, the parakeet is not going to just hop onto your finger right away. You also have to be ready for a nip or two if you try to get close to your bird too soon. Eventually the bird will come to know you, and you can place your finger under its chest. Though it may still nip you at this point, the bird will soon be hopping onto your finger.

Parakeets are friendly pets.

Parakeets are much easier to manage if their wings are clipped. You might want to ask the pet store manager or bird breeder to explain to you how to clip wings safely, or to do it for you.

Parakeets, tamed and well cared for, become comfortable around people. These birds will eat from your hand and sit on your arm, finger, or shoulder.

21

Pet stores sell special seeds for both canaries and parakeets. You can also feed these birds fresh greens. Canaries, in particular, like sprouted seeds. Give fresh water and food daily.

For canaries and parakeets you need a standard medium-sized birdcage (about eighteen inches high and wide). Both canaries and parakeets need to be kept warm and protected from drafts. Cover your bird's cage at night. Give fresh water and food daily.

Clean the cage thoroughly once a week, and line the cage bottom with fresh paper every day. Birds also need a piece of cuttlebone—sold in pet stores—to keep their beaks in shape. Parakeets and canaries like to take splash baths. Put a saucer of water in the cage every couple of days, and remove it after your bird has enjoyed its bath.

Always cover a birdcage at night to protect your bird from drafts.

6

Fish

You can't take a fish out for a walk on a leash, and a fish won't come and sit on your finger either. Yet fish as pets can be wonderful for stimulating the imagination or for just plain watching. Remember that they live in the world of water while you live in the world of air. They are mysterious because they seem so distant.

Keeping fish can begin as an inexpensive pastime, but it can grow into an elaborate and time-consuming hobby. On the inexpensive side are common goldfish and guppies. On the more expensive side are the many varieties of tropical fish.

For goldfish and guppies you need a five-and-a-half gallon tank or a wide-mouthed bowl. Either of these will allow enough contact between air and water. With enough contact, there will be enough oxygen for one or two fish to breathe.

Tropical fish require a tank with pump, filter, and other equipment.

The many beautiful varieties of tropical fish are fascinating to watch.

23

GOLDFISH

There are different varieties of goldfish. The most common is called the "Comet." Others include the "Fantail" and the "Black Moor." All are inexpensive.

Goldfish are hearty and some have lived up to fifty years in captivity, though ten years is a more reasonable maximum life span.

When buying a goldfish, make sure that you get one that is healthy. If a fish looks weak and is not active, it probably should not even be in the pet store tank. You don't want a fish like that. Check the tail fins for damage or disease. And there should be no waste trailing from the tail of the fish. When you point out the healthy fish you want to the salesperson, make sure that is the one you get.

You will probably leave the store with the fish in a little plastic bag filled with water. There is not much air in the bag, so get the fish into its new home right away. But don't just dump it into a bowl full of cold water. Before you leave home to purchase the fish, fill up one or more gallon jugs with water so that the water will come to room temperature. Goldfish can handle fairly cool temperatures, but not all of a sudden.

If you do not use a filter system, you must clean the tank or bowl at least once a week. The safe way to do this is to drain water from the bowl or tank, using a small pump or plastic hose. If you use a hose to drain the tank, draw a little water halfway up the hose from the tank by putting your mouth at the other end of the hose and breathing in slightly. Be careful not to sip any water into your mouth. Then place the end of the hose downward into a pail. The water will flow out of the tank above into the empty pail below. This is called "siphoning." Do not remove all of the water from the tank. Leave enough to allow your fish to continue to swim along the bottom.

After the dirty water has run out into a pail, use the pump or hose to "vacuum" the dirt from the bottom of the tank. The siphon hose removes dirt just as easily as it removes water. While the water is low, use a wet sponge (no soap!) to clean the inside glass of the tank or bowl. Much less siphoning and cleaning is required when you use a filter system for the tank. With a filter, you need to siphon only once a month.

Cleaning the bowl or tank is the hardest part of caring for a goldfish. Feeding them is easy. Goldfish can live very well on the goldfish food

With good care, goldfish can live ten years or more. 25

sold in pet stores. Sprinkle a tiny bit into the bowl or tank once or twice a day. If they finish the food, sprinkle a tiny bit more. But don't feed them too much! Too much leftover food creates an unhealthy tank.

GUPPIES

You can easily become a fish breeder if you choose a pair of guppies for pets. A healthy male and female will quickly produce plenty of babies for all to admire. When you pick out a pair of guppies, remember that females have fat bellies with a dark spot. Males are slender. Get one of each, and put some plants and rocks in the tank for the young guppies to hide behind.

Guppies need a tank with a filter system.

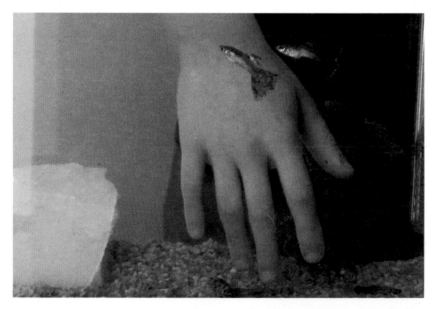

Fancy guppies should be kept in a heated tank.

They also need a warmer and more constant water temperature than goldfish. Depending on how warm it is in your home, you may need to purchase an aquarium heater to keep the temperature in the tank above sixty degrees.

If you succeed with goldfish or guppies, and enjoy fish in general, you may want to try keeping tropical fish.

You will need a tank that will hold at least ten gallons of water, and special equipment, plants, and decorations. If you are interested, make a trip to an aquarium supply store and look at the many types of fish and kinds of equipment available. Talk with the salesperson about what you will need to get started.

You may have a promising future as a tropical fish hobbyist!

The red-eyed tetra is a popular tropical fish.

7

Dogs

Dogs are loving and loyal. They are smart and attentive. But they also require a lot of care and training, more than any other pet in this book.

The best place to get a free or inexpensive mixed-breed puppy (a puppy whose parents are of different breeds) is from people with a young litter (a family of newborn pups). Pups from a good home are more likely to turn out to be good pets, so it is important to visit the litters a few weeks before it is time to select a pup.

How can you decide which is the right dog for you? When you visit, observe the tempera-

This puppy was adopted from the ASPCA—the American Society for the Prevention of Cruelty to Animals.

This puppy, like many mixed-breed dogs, is attractive and appealing.

28

Food, water, and a comfortable bed make a nice den for a new puppy.

ment of the mother dog and the way she looks after her pups. If she is timid and inattentive, her pups may not turn out to be happy dogs. Ask the owners if they handle the pups. It is important that they do, because early handling helps the pups get used to people.

When choosing a puppy, handle each candidate yourself. A psychologically healthy puppy is eager to meet you. It does not back off in fear, and it does not timidly roll over on its back as it approaches you. Once you have its attention, a pup should want to follow you and come to you when you call it by gently clapping your hands together.

The physical signs of a healthy puppy are a good smell, clear eyes, a shiny coat, and a little plumpness. Look carefully for these things. Try not to let your emotions lead you to choose a pup that you feel sorry for. Chances are you'll be sorrier if you make it your pet.

The time to visit a litter is when the pups are two months old. Your puppy will still be too young to come home with you then. But after another month, the pup you choose will no longer need its mother and should be ready to come home with you.

29

There are several things you must do both before and after the new member of your household arrives. You must take your puppy to a vet for its first series of shots and a general examination. Have a bed, water bowl, food bowl, and puppy food ready for your pet. It also needs a collar and leash.

Place your puppy's bed and bowls near one another in an area covered with several layers of newspaper. The newspaper is the puppy's

Just like you, dogs are happiest when they get a lot of love and affection.

bathroom. Leash the puppy to something that will not move. For now you do not want the puppy to roam off the newspaper.

A puppy is always sad to be separated from its family. So from the moment you bring it home until your puppy gets over the pain of leaving its first home (which takes at least a few days), it will probably be miserable. Just try to make your puppy comfortable during this time. Speak sweetly and softly. Pet the puppy gently and often. But don't expect it to play. Puppies play when they are happy.

At night, equip your puppy's bed with a hot-water bottle and a ticking clock. The bottle and clock will often make the young animal feel more comfortable during those first long nights away from the family it has left.

Treat your puppy with great care and a lot of attention during these first few days. It will soon become your devoted pet.

HOUSEBREAKING

The most difficult task confronting you now is the long process of housebreaking. It takes at least one month, usually three, sometimes six. You've got to have determination and patience and a willingness to sacrifice your time.

To begin the process, confine the puppy to an area covered with newspapers. Each time the pup uses the paper, throw the paper into the outdoor garbage and replace it with a fresh layer. Meanwhile, take the puppy outside several times a day. The most important part of your job is to give the puppy every opportunity to go to the bathroom outdoors.

Take the puppy out early in the morning (get up earlier than you normally would). Also take it out right after every meal and every time it starts to sniff around suspiciously. Then take the puppy out before you go to bed. In addition to these suggested times, take it out whenever you have a spare moment.

When your puppy does mess on the floor

or rug, punish it only when you've caught it in the act. Grab the extra fur at the back of its neck and give it a firm shake, raising your voice so that you sound slightly harsh. Then take your puppy outside as soon as possible. If you don't catch your puppy in the act or shortly afterward, forget the punishment. The puppy probably won't get the point. In this case, all you can do is clean up the mess.

Whenever it does go to the bathroom outside, immediately praise and pet your pup. *Eventually* the dog learns that you think it is wonderful when it goes outside and not-so-wonderful when it goes indoors. Remember—you will not have an overnight success. As it grows older and you have more confidence in your pet, the number of times it must be walked every day will go down, possibly to as few as four.

Cleaning up your puppy's messes is your responsibility. Don't expect someone else to do it for you.

FEEDING

A puppy loves to eat. It will want its dry puppy food at least three times a day, sometimes even four. (Moisten the dry food with warm water, and add a dash of canned food.) As it grows older, cut the feedings back to twice a day. When your pup reaches its first birthday, feed it adult dry dog food once a day. Continue to add canned food. Always keep your pup's water bowl filled with fresh water, and rinse the food bowl out after each meal.

GROOMING

Both puppies and grown dogs need to be brushed and sometimes combed. How often depends on the dog's coat. Short hair needs brushing once a week. Long hair needs brushing twice a week.

When you introduce a puppy to brushing, it may not like being brushed. Speak gently to your puppy, no matter how much it squirms and yelps. Try to remain calm. Your puppy will get used to being brushed if you do it often enough. Praise your puppy and reward it after the brushing. Your puppy will appreciate it, and learn to cooperate.

TRAINING

Besides learning to go to the bathroom outdoors, dogs must learn a lot of other things. They must learn *not* to bite, *not* to go into the garbage for a snack, *not* to jump up on people, *not* to

33

climb on furniture, and *not* to take food away from people. To teach these things, you have to use firm voice commands, firm gestures and—rarely—a firm slap. If you are always kind and gentle and affectionate, your dog will get the message when you discipline it. If your dog bites you or if you catch it doing something else wrong, raise your voice and say "No!"

Don't overdo discipline. The dog will eventually become aware of what pleases you. The more you treat your dog with affection, the more

The first step in your dog's training is teaching it to sit.

it will notice scolding. If you are always yelling at and hitting your dog, it may just get used to being scolded and come to expect it as a way of life. Your dog might even start to be naughty as an act of defiance.

Another important kind of training involves only reward and no discipline. All dogs should sit, lie down, and stay when they are told. And all dogs should know how to walk on a leash, even if they live in the country.

As always, be patient. It takes time for a

All dogs should learn to walk properly on a leash. The command is "heel."

dog to learn the meaning of a command word. To teach a dog how to sit, say the word "sit" as you put your dog in that position by holding your dog's chest and pushing its rear down. Any signs of progress should be praised. Your dog will enjoy the praise and will be more cooperative. Teach your dog to "lie down" and "stay" using the same method. Any time your pup obeys a command without needing much help from you, it deserves a treat as a reward.

Learning to walk properly on a leash is something all dogs should learn. Once again, you must be patient and persistent. Learn how to use a leash and slip collar, a special chain collar for training your dog. A slip collar will tighten around the dog's neck when you jerk on the leash, and loosen when you stop pulling. When the dog rushes ahead of you, jerk back firmly on the leash. Jerking on the leash will bring the dog back to your side. The slip collar will loosen when your dog remains walking right at your side, and your dog will once again be comfortable. Your dog will need hours of practice in the yard to learn to walk by your side on a leash without guidance from you.

The command for walking at your side is "Heel!" If you occasionally mix in other easier commands it already understands, that will help the dog realize that you are teaching it something.

Always remember that dogs are not as smart as people, and that they don't think and understand the way we do. Always be kind and affectionate. If you treat your dog badly, it may become a badly behaved pet. Patience and praise will help your dog learn, and keep it happy.

8

Turtles, Salamanders, and Snakes

Turtles, snakes, and salamanders can each be housed in a fish tank, but only the turtle requires enough water in which to swim.

TURTLES

When you go shopping for a turtle, look for one that is lively and pay close attention to how well it swims. Don't buy a sluggish turtle. And avoid turtles with swollen eyelids or with white patches of fungus on their skin.

Turtles love to swim, especially since they eat all of their meals in the water. But they also need some high ground on which to dry out. By

Turtles need a place to swim, and a place to dry out.

37

drying out, they avoid contracting a fungus that can make them sick. An aquarium one-third to one-half full of water provides an adequate swimming area. The high ground can be created by piling up smooth stones that rise up out of the water.

A turtle will climb up onto a rock to get its daily dose of light. You have to provide light in the form of an ultra-violet fluorescent bulb. Turtles like warmth, so keep the light on throughout the day. In fact, temperatures much below eighty degrees slow turtles down to the point where they don't eat. The special light, which feels like sunshine to the turtle, will keep your pet healthy and alert.

Turtles eat many things, including dried insects and insect eggs, which can be purchased at pet stores. Green vegetables like lettuce, and bits of meat and fish are also good for turtles. They also need extra calcium in powder form, available at pet and drug stores.

SALAMANDERS

There are many types of salamanders. You can check to see if a pet store has any in stock. But if you live near the woods, it may be more fun to find one on your own.

Salamanders always need to be moist, so they are usually found in damp spots. Try turning over a dead log or a rock, or lifting a patch of dead leaves with a stick. Of course, be very careful if you live in an area where there are snakes.

You can make a home for a salamander

in a partially-filled fish tank. Add a pile of rocks in one corner of the tank for "sunning." Or fill the tank with earth and a sunken, deep dish of water. Put a sturdy fish-tank cover on top of the tank so that the inside will remain humid. The salamander's environment needs to be kept moist, so if your tank is mostly filled with earth, spray it with mist about once a week. You can buy a spray-mist bottle in a hardware or garden supply store. Lift the tank cover for about a half-hour every day to let in fresh air, and clean the water dish each week. The mostly water-filled tanks should have a fish-tank kind of filter.

Salamanders eat mostly small insects. Start

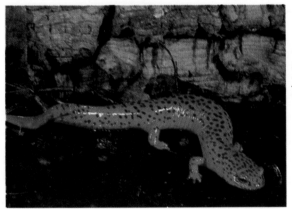

Salamanders like to stay moist. Sometimes you can find them underneath wet leaves.

a colony of fruit flies in a jar and transfer a fresh supply into the salamander's tank each week. The tank cover will prevent the fruit flies from escaping from the tank.

SNAKES

Don't expect your parents to be thrilled if you tell them you want a pet snake. Snakes are among the most feared animals in the world.   **39**

Strangely enough, they make good pets and are easy to take care of. But don't go out into the woods to trap your own snake. Buy one of the varieties sold in pet stores, such as a corn snake.

There are two important things to consider when selecting a snake for a pet. First, is it eating well? This is a sure sign of good health. Ask the pet store manager about this. Second, can the pet store manager pick up the snake without the snake getting mad? This is a test for tameness. Hostile snakes are not fun to handle or keep, and they make people nervous.

The corn snake makes a good pet.

Snakes live a simple life. Give them a clean tank with newspaper covering the bottom. They need a dark hide-out, which can be a cardboard box or even a paper bag. And they need a bowl of water to drink from and a branch on which to climb. To keep the snake from getting out of the tank, cover the tank with a wire mesh and weigh down the mesh with something reasonably heavy.

Finally, snakes eat live food. Mice, frogs, fish, and earthworms are among the meals preferred by different snakes.

9

Exotic pets

If you have an urge for a pet that's really something out of the ordinary, consider these three. Ferrets, parrots, and iguanas are not common household pets. Yet each has special qualities that will fascinate you.

FERRETS

In the wild the ferret is a hunter, but it can be a good pet. If you purchase one when it is young, just after being weaned, a ferret can be handled and petted so that it grows up tame and

Ferrets love to play and make good pets.

41

friendly. Don't get a ferret at an older age because it may already have developed wild habits it can't break. Also, a female ferret is less likely to run away when it grows up than a male ferret. If you do get a male, have it neutered if you want to keep it around.

You can let a tame ferret roam free in your house. But keep it in a cage until you are confident that it is friendly and comfortable in your home. Inside the cage, provide a closed-off den—an old wooden box or crate with a hole for a door—where the ferret can go to sleep. Also provide the ferret with a litter box inside the cage (ferrets need pretty big cages—approximately two feet by three feet minimum). If the ferret uses another spot inside the cage for a bathroom, move the litter box to that spot and hope for the best. Clean the cage twice a week.

Ferrets live well on canned cat food, and they need a constant supply of fresh water.

PARROTS

Think carefully before you consider hav-

Parrots like to get to know their owners.

Parrots are more expensive than most pets, but they can live for fifty years.

ing a pet parrot. First, a parrot lives a long time, often fifty years or longer. Second, a parrot that won't be tamed is scary and dangerous. So be careful in choosing and training this kind of bird. A tame parrot can make a beautiful and affectionate pet.

Parrots are expensive. Many are two hundred dollars or more. If the price is not too high for you, how do you choose the right parrot for you?

Try to find out about the parrot's temperament. How does it react to your hand moving close to its cage? If it panics and starts screeching, don't buy it. If it just acts timid and backs off, proceed. Ask the pet store salesperson to handle the parrot and give you a demonstration. If the salesperson won't or can't handle the parrot, that's a bad sign. The parrot has not been handled enough, and you will have a difficult time trying to tame it.

A parrot is not fun to have as a pet if it   **43**

has to spend all of its many years inside a cage. It has to be tamable so that it can come outside the cage to sit on your shoulder, and have a chance to rub its head against your neck.

Here is one more tip. Get the largest cage you can find, because a parrot is a big bird and needs plenty of room to stretch its wings. The parrot cage itself is expensive.

You can purchase parrot food from pet stores. The parrot's diet can also include fresh greens, some fruit, and some crushed oyster shells for minerals. A parrot must have fresh water every day.

Taming a parrot is similar to taming a parakeet, except that it can be about three times as difficult. The reason it is harder is that a parrot can hurt you if it is upset. Before you even bring a parrot home, make sure that its wings are clipped at the pet store. If its wings are clipped, it won't be able to fly for a while. (Don't try to clip the parrot's wings yourself.)

At the beginning, do not try to get a parrot to hop onto your bare finger. Use a wood stick instead. The parrot first needs time to get used to having the stick in its cage. Read one or more of the books available on parrot training. Remember, though, that there is no substitute for being gentle and kind.

IGUANAS

Because iguanas look like dragons, they may frighten some people. These unusual animals also grow up to be quite big, as much as a few feet in length, which means their tanks have to be large and tall.

Because iguanas come from the tropics or deserts, they need warm temperatures. Tropical iguanas also need lots of humidity. You can maintain a warm temperature in your iguana tank with an ultra-violet fluorescent bulb. And you can maintain the humidity with a built-in pool of water, which must be changed each day. Never close off the air in a tank because stagnant, hot, humid air promotes disease. A weighted-down, wire-mesh cover is the answer.

The iguana's favorite foods are fresh fruits and greens (lettuce, carrot tops, leafy vegetables). They like to eat a lot. Remove leftovers and droppings from the tank every day.

Iguanas like to stay warm, because they come from deserts and the tropics.

10

Multiple Pets

Like many people, you may really want to own a dog. But it may be impossible because of where you live, or because you can't convince the rest of the family that it is a good idea.

One way to get over your disappointment is to have more than one pet. You can do this even if you do own a dog. Just make sure that you "check your schedule" first, talk with your parents, and

Here are two pets that get along very well.

don't commit yourself to more pet chores than you can handle.

Pay attention to good and bad combinations when you select an additional pet. Cats love mice, but they love them the way you love ice cream. A cat and a dog sometimes get along, but **46** not always.

On the other hand, a guinea pig and a goldfish never have arguments. The same goes for a rabbit and a hamster.

Be sure not to expose an animal to one of its natural predators, or enemies. But if you do keep two or more pets that are not entirely friendly to one another, it is your duty to protect the weaker one and to care for all equally.

Pets need your care and love. They can be wonderful friends. Whether you have one pet or several, the experience will add a great deal of interest and joy to your life.

INDEX

EAU CLAIRE DISTRICT LIBRARY